From Owner to Professional Management: Problems in Transition

The Conference Board

ABOUT THE CONFERENCE BOARD

The Conference Board is a business information service whose purpose is to assist senior executives and other leaders in arriving at sound decisions. Since its founding in 1916, the Board has been creating close personal networks of leaders who exchange experience and judgment on significant issues in management practice, economics and public policy. The networks are supported by an international program of research and meetings which The Conference Board staff of more than 350 persons carries out from offices in New York, Ottawa and Brussels.

More than 3,600 organizations in over 50 nations participate in The Conference Board's work as Associates. The Board is a not-for-profit corporation and the greatest share of its financial support comes from business concerns, many with worldwide operations. The Board also has many Associates among labor unions, colleges and universities, government agencies, libraries and trade and professional associations.

The Conference Board, Inc.
845 Third Avenue
New York, New York 10022
(212) 759-0900
RCA International Telex
237282 and 234465

The Conference Board, Inc.
Avenue Louise, 207 - Bte 5
B-1050 Brussels, Belgium
(02) 640 62 40
Telex: 63635

The Conference Board, Inc.
1755 Massachusetts Avenue, N.W.
Suite 312
Washington, D.C. 20036
(202) 483-0580

The Conference Board of Canada
25 McArthur Road
Suite 100
Ottawa, Ontario, K1L-6R3
(613) 746-1261

Conference Board Report No. 851   Printed in U.S.A.

ISBN NO.: 0-8237 0292-8

WITHDRAWN

From Owner to Professional Management: Problems in Transition

by Ronald E. Berenbeim

A Research Report from the Conference Board

Contents

Exhibits

Chart

Author's Acknowledgments

The following individuals were generous with their time in discussing the issues that are explored in detail: Ivan Lansberg H., an International Counsellor of The Conference Board; members of The Conference Board's Executive Council and Mauricio Brehm of the Instituo Panamericano de Alta Direccion de Estudios (IPADE).

Salvador Zuniga of Mexico City and Malcolm Brooks of The Conference Board in Europe gave indispensable help in arranging interviews with Mexican and European participants.

Within The Conference Board, Elizabeth A. Duman coordinated clerical support and Martha Parra and Margarita Wells provided Spanish language assistance.

As in the past, the author profited from the helpful editorial comments of Harold Stieglitz, then the Board's Vice President for Europe. The manuscript was edited by Lillian W. Kay, Manager, Editorial Services, and Joyce Fine Schultz, Senior Editorial Associate.

Why This Report

Company founders tell us how concerned they are at the risks that lie in wait for their businesses when they retire. By all accounts the departure of the founder is an emotionally charged event, and one which, depending on how well it is handled, can critically affect the future of the company. This report is a response to the request of CEOs—in the United States, Europe, and Latin America—for an exploration of this transition from owner to professional management.

It explores how founders prepare themselves and their associates for this transition. It examines how founders withdraw from day-to-day management while still retaining power to make those crucial decisions that shape the company's long-term interests. It analyzes how relations between the other major players in the founder's family, the founding coalition, and the company's professional management are tested and, in many instances, dramatically redefined. It looks at the institutional and personal mechanisms founders use to introduce new leadership while ensuring continuity and achieving a smooth transition. This study focuses on how 20 U.S., Latin American, and European companies addressed the often conflicting needs of founders, their families, and company employees.

We are grateful to all the founders, family members, and professional managers in the United States, Latin America, and Europe who shared their views with us.

JAMES T. MILLS
President

Chapter 1

The Family Company: Evolutionary Stages and Problems of Passage

FORD AND DUPONT are only two of the major public-ly owned business organizations that bear a family name. Over the years, these firms and thousands of others have evolved from small founder- or family-dominated com-panies to professionally managed business institutions. This process was easier to accomplish in some cases than in others.

The transitional stages and key periods of crisis through which these companies passed occur in many kinds of business organizations. But the fact of family involvement—and later disengagement—gives special em-phasis to some of the critical factors that most companies confront in effecting substantial changes in direction and in management processes.

Any company that is currently adjusting to a new CEO or to the implementation of new systems and procedures can look at the transitional stages of a family-owned com-pany for vivid examples of what does or does not work; the recollections of founders and heirs with recent ex-periences underscore this relevance.

Among the problems with which the family corporation must cope, those most pertinent to the process of organiza-tional change, are:

(1) Institutionalizing "professional management" systems;

(2) Providing for adequate internal management succes-sion with—or, at some point, without—family involvement; and

(3) Ensuring sufficient family guidance and control when the founder or family leaves active operational management.

This study discusses the measures that participants took in advancing toward their objectives. Where the companies failed, those interviewed were asked why they thought this had been the outcome. Invariably, when this has hap-pened, the company reverted to a squabbling coalition that lacked the effective mediating abilities of the founder. In some instances, the pieces were put back together and the company regained lost ground in progressing toward a business institution. Other companies never recovered from this institutional trauma.

The Family-Owned Company: Early Stages of Development

For analytical purposes, the growth and development of any family-owned company can be viewed as going through three or, sometimes, four stages.[1] At each stage, the founder, the family, and the company will have different needs and relationships with respect to one another. (See Chart 1.) Each of the first two stages of development has its own particular problems of passage that can impede the company's evolution to institutional maturity. The effort to resolve these developmental problems can precipitate an institutional crisis, but study participants agree on the need for resolution if the company is to progress to the next stage. The principal characteristics of each phase and the major evolutionary task are characterized below.

(1) *Coalition:* To establish the company, the founder builds a coalition of diverse supporters. Each brings a necessary ingredient to the situation, and is induced to make a financial or personal contribution by the prospect of some kind of reward. Typically, this venture will include some, or all, of the following:

- *Financial backers,* who lend money at a favorable rate of interest, or at no interest at all;
- *Highly skilled employees,* who may contribute their skills at a lower rate of compensation than they might com-mand elsewhere;
- *Other family members,* who defer the security and well-being that could be theirs if the founder were to work as a salaried employee of an established firm;
- *Suppliers of goods and services,* who provide materials or services (including professional services); and
- *Customers,* who place orders at the outset and, in so doing, give the enterprise an early viability.

---

[1] Many commentators have analyzed the various stages of development of small businesses and entrepreneurial companies. These categories are not devised as an effort to participate in that discussion. Their purpose is to describe the changing roles and attitudes of the founder and the family and how these changes affect management processes within the company.

Chart 1: Needs and Relationships of the Parties

CATEGORY STAGE OF DEVELOPMENT	FOUNDER — Needs	FOUNDER — Relationship to Other Elements	FAMILY — Needs	FAMILY — Relationship to Other Elements	COMPANY — Needs	COMPANY — Relationship to Other Elements
COALITION	Alliances with: (1) Financial backers (2) Highly skilled employees (3) Suppliers (includes services, e.g., lawyers, accountants) (4) Customers (5) Other family members	(1) Conceives product or service. (2) Articulates family and business objectives. (3) Develops structure of company. (4) Acts as broker between competing interests of coalition members. (5) Provides for welfare of individual family members.	(1) Economic needs are moderate. (2) Company is the sole source of family income and employment.	(1) Family may be involved in functional and policy aspects of the business. (2) Family acts both inside and outside the company to support the founder.	Has the same alliances as the founder does. However, at this point, the coalition partners are committed personally to the founder rather than to the company.	(1) Subordinate to the founder for both policy and functional leadership. (2) A source of employment for family members.
FOUNDER ASCENDANT	(1) Highly skilled and experienced heads of functional departments (2) Support for personal vision of the future from Board of Directors (3) Family commitment to his or her extensive involvement in the firm	(1) Makes important day-to-day operational decisions for the company. (2) Sets economic priorities within the family and provides for individual needs of family members.	(1) Economic needs are high. (2) Economic priorities may differ significantly among members. Emphasis is on a balance between income and capital appreciation. (3) Company is the primary if not exclusive source of family wealth. (4) Company may be source of captive employment for family.	(1) Family defers to founder on company policy issues. (2) Family works in company on an as needed rather than meritocratic basis. (3) Supports founder in his or her heavy commitment to company.	(1) High degree of functional expertise (2) Overall guidance from founder for objectives and policy (3) Inventory of personal and organizational: (a) strategies (b) skills (c) relationships.	(1) Subordinate to founder for both functional and policy guidelines. (2) Family members have an advantage in obtaining employment with company. Once hired they are judged on merit.
BUSINESS INSTITUTION	(1) Well articulated statement of company mission and purpose (2) Effective mechanisms within company for transferrence of skills and sharing of experience (3) Systems and procedures that enable the company to function without day-to-day involvement in decision making	(1) Sets overall objectives and policy for company and family. (2) Represents and promotes interests of both company and family within the community. (3) Mediates disputes within both company and family.	(1) Economic needs are high and varied because: (a) family is large (b) some members seek growth; others want income or security (2) Conflict between needs; members promote their own objectives: (a) income (b) capital appreciation (c) security (d) employment.	(1) Family seeks sharing of power with founder to define family and company objectives. (2) Members may be involved in company as: (a) employees (b) policymakers (directors) or (c) investors (3) Family has diversified sources of employment and income. Does not rely on the company exclusively for either.	(1) Policy guidance (2) Important ties to community and industry (connectional assets) (3) Effective mechanisms for the transfer of skills and the sharing of experience (4) Ability to function without the founder's day-to-day involvement	(1) Provides the founder with effective support in his or her promotion of the company mission within the industry and the community. (2) Supplies the founder with adequate information to define overall objectives and policy. (3) Strikes appropriate balance between competing family needs for: (a) income (b) capital appreciation (c) financial security (d) employment.

The Participants

As most of the world's enterprises—even the larger ones—are family-owned or dominated, the potential list of participants is virtually coextensive with all the enterprises in the United States, Latin America, and Europe.

However, a large proportion of these family businesses—indeed most businesses—are not really *business organizations*. Rather, they are single proprietorships—retail outlets or concerns that provide services to the community or neghborhood. An extremely small percentage requires some form of production, financial, sales and marketing management. Of this group, only a minority has resolved, or will resolve, the various institutional "crises" that are the subject of this study. They will grow into ongoing business institutions that survive the founder's retirement and generate growth and opportunity through institutional effort. Of these, a handful will become the IBM's, Fords or Philipses of the future.

The 20 U.S., Latin American, and European companies that participated in this study are all well-established ongoing concerns. Median annual sales for the group are well over $100 million and, in a few cases, sales exceed $1 billion. The substantial family presence is evident in a variety of ways. It often takes the form of ownership of a large block of stock (not necessarily over 50 percent). In other instances, the family has kept a modest ownership position while still playing an oversight or management role. Whatever form family participation takes, the key is that the destinies of the family and the company are indissolubly linked in the minds of family members, employees and the general public.

Although they constitute a diverse group with respect to size, age and industry, all of the companies reported on here have certain common characteristics:

(1) They were founded by a single person or by a group of people who remain active in the company, or whose family or families continue to be involved in the company (beyond the mere ownership of shares) after the departure of the founder(s).

(2) They are developing, or have succeeded in establishing, principles and systems that provide continuity in management and in the criteria for the choice of business alternatives.

(3) The family, or group of families, that is involved in the company is able to train and select heirs for appropriate roles in the firm.

Companies from six countries were studied—six in the United States; five in Mexico; four in Belgium; two each in France, and the United Kingdom; and one in Venezuela. Founders, professional managers and heirs were interviewed. In a number of instances, information about a company was obtained from more than one source.

Owners were asked questions relating to company history, succession and the introduction of professional management. Professional managers talked about their backgrounds, training and experience, how they had been recruited, and the allocation of authority between them and the family. Heirs commented on the degree to which founders shared information about the company with the family, and discussed the problems that arose between themselves and founders or long-time employees. In addition to discussion of these company-related concerns, views were solicited from all participants as to special cultural and economic circumstances that affected the transition from owner to professional management and almost everyone discussed the role of government.

The major developmental task in the coalition phase is to establish the legitimacy of the founder to lead the organization and to act on its behalf without interference from other coalition members. The one point on which all participants generally agreed is the way in which this is accomplished: Growth and success are the only means available to the founder to achieve freedom of action. Without it, there will be a continuing need for external financing, keeping both founder and company subject to the constraints that lenders impose on borrowers. Without growth, it can also be more difficult to attract and motivate highly qualified employees.

(2) *Founder ascendant:* Once the founder's authority and freedom to act have been established, the company evolves to what might be called the founder-ascendant organization. The founder charts the course for the firm and is an indispensable party to all important decisions. Whether they go or stay, the original coalition members accept the fact that the founder's intense involvement will keep them from playing major roles, at least for the present.

The key institutional objective of this second stage is to establish the legitimacy of the organization to act with or without the participation of the founder in management decisions. Those interviewed agreed that this is accomplished by:

- Recruitment of individuals with needed management as well as functional skills;
- Delegation of important decision-making authority by the founder to other senior managers;
- Development of procedural mechanisms for making important decisions within the company;
- Establishment of controls for monitoring the implementation of decisions; and
- Determination of the part that the founder's family will play in the company's future, in both managerial and ownership roles. In the first instance, it raises the question of whether the family has suitable candidates for top managerial posts. In the second case, the family will determine whether it wants to share ownership with the public.

Chapter 2

The Rules of The Game: Becoming a Business Institution

NEGOTIATING THE DIFFICULT passage from coalition to founder ascendance requires business skills, achieving growth and making money. The transition from a founder-ascendant company to a business institution raises *management* issues. To the founder or the family oriented primarily toward entrepreneurial or functional activities, this imposes a whole set of more formidable demands. Study participants emphasized that certain pragmatic considerations were necessary to achieve these ends.

It is necessary to have heirs, although not too many. To perpetuate family control of a company, heirs are needed to inherit the business (but not so many as to dilute and ultimately paralyze their ability to manage). The first requirement for those who plan to achieve continuity through family participation is to have enough children interested in the business and to provide a range of talent. Each heir is then prepared over a period of years for company (and family) leadership.

Among those interviewed who had especially grand designs for their firms, there was a realization that one family might not be enough. These individuals felt it necessary to knit the families of early financial backers, suppliers and loyal employees into the fabric of their companies. A high-level executive with a large British retail enterprise that has been run by a single family for nearly a century observed that heirs were a critical factor in preserving continuity: "This was a large family. At any one time in the company's history there were always a large number of heirs who were willing to and capable of assuming important posts."

A corollary to this view is the proposition that there can be too many heirs. The founding family of a European chemical company had so many heirs by the fourth generation that the diversity of views and interests of the group were indistinguishable from those of the public at large. This is likely to be a long-term problem for any family. However, if there is a proliferation of heirs before the company has become an effective ongoing institution, the family may not succeed in stamping the company with a coherent identity.

Avoid confusion of family and company roles. When management succession entails the transition of power from the founder to a son or daughter, there is, typically, a reluctance on the part of the elder person to retreat to a more modest role. Retiring while still relatively vigorous and able to supply counsel and assistance when it is sought, is a sound principle for a founder who wants the family business to survive. Heads of large family businesses that remained successful in succeeding generations all noted that their predecessors had created an orderly and gradual transition—one marked by a willingness to let their successors try and even fail in important positions, and ultimately to retire so that a new generation could take over without interference.

The company clearly states basic principles of obligation to the community, customers and employees. Leaders of businesses that have survived often point to a well-conceived sense of mission linking the business to values and objectives that are more fundamental than simple insistence on a bottom-line profit or on providing for the security of family members. These individuals question the chance for long-term survival where the company's sole objective is the generation of wealth. In their view, the company gains legitimacy and support through the promotion of its beliefs.

Many family firms in the United States, Latin America, and Europe have devoted considerable effort to explaining these fundamental principles in writing. (See Exhibits 1 and 2.) The statements are often rooted in the deep convictions of the founder, and are used to set rules for dealing with the community, customers and employees. In so doing, they provide assurance that the firm will not sacrifice long-term relationships, and the values on which they are based, for short-term profits.

The heirs undergo rigorous training to assume their responsibilities. When the leader of a Belgian firm was asked to tick off the requirements for a family member who wished to participate in the company, he cited: four languages; business and engineering degrees; and, if possible, work experience in the United States. These kinds of

Exhibit 1: A U.S. Manufacturer: Statement of Corporate Purpose, Values and Beliefs

> Yarway Corporation exists to serve people throughout the world by supplying excellent products and services to those basic industries which meet human needs for electricity, heat, fuel, chemicals, paper, food, fibers, transportation and pollution control.
>
> Excellence and integrity in all that we do.
> Worthwhile social contributions.
> Worldwide scope of activities and attitudes.
> Self-determination with appropriate accountability.

prerequisites serve two purposes. First, they prepare the individual for the job. Second, and perhaps more important, they confer *legitimacy*.

Inheritors, by definition, achieve their positions through birth; they do not earn them through merit. But heirs can acquire *legitimacy* through their achievements in other institutions, where they must compete on an equal basis with many individuals. Legitimacy, in turn, achieves two important objectives: Other employees have greater respect for the heirs, and the heirs develop greater confidence in their own abilities. The latter, more than the need for experience, is probably the reason why so many founders insist that

their heirs have some record of achievement outside the family business.

In many instances, heirs are required to earn their way inside the company as well. After his return from the Korean War, Otis Chandler, the heir to the Los Angeles *Times,* was presented with a seven-year work program that required experience in the press, mail and city rooms, and in the advertising department. He started the following Monday. The mailers were so pleased with his performance that he was voted "Apprentice Most Likely to Succeed."[1] This illustrates a fairly common practice among study participants.

From Rule to Reign

Although the previously stated principles are critical, the most significant task confronting the family is the uncoupling of proprietary from managerial concerns. When successful, it allows the firm's professional managers to function effectively in their individual capacities while protecting the rights of owners to participate in decisions that cannot be delegated to employees.

For every family firm that has become an institution, there comes a time when the family has to give up day-to-day

---

[1]David Halberstam, *The Powers that Be.* New York: Alfred A. Knopf, 1979 p. 98.

Exhibit 2: A Simple Approach: Marks and Spencer Human Philosophy[1]

> We offer our customers a selective range of high-quality well-designed and attractive merchandise at reasonable prices under our brand name 'St. Michael.'
>
> We foster good human relations with customers, suppliers and staff, and the communities in which we trade. We believe that people come first and that if you treat people decently and with humanity, the vast majority respond. We put our trust in our management—who are there because they are able to make a sensible decision—and our staff, most of whom are devoted people. We rely on common sense and do not try to legislate for exceptions. We take all our management and staff into our confidence. This is the foundation of our success and is an area to which the executive Board devotes much time and expense. We are leaders in the proper treatment of people.
>
> We encourage our suppliers to use the most modern and efficient techniques of production available from the latest developments in technology.
>
> With the cooperation of our suppliers, we work to ensure the highest standards of quality control.
>
> We plan the expansion of our stores for the better display of a widening range of goods and for the convenience of our customers.
>
> We aim to simplify operating procedures so that our business is carried on in the most efficient manner. We have in a large degree a personal business with good communications between people and the minimum of bureaucracy and as little paperwork as is possible with the statutory requirements. Paperwork and statistical information multiplies if unchecked, stands in the way of proper contact between people, whether customers, suppliers or staff. We rely on people, not reports.
>
> [1]From a speech by Jan de Somogyi, Economic Adviser to the Board of Directors of Marks and Spencer, p.l.c., to the Retail Research Society, City University of New York.

management control of the company. In many of the companies participating in this study, the power had already passed to professional managers. The transition to professional management had often occurred when the family had no suitable candidate to succeed the founder. In a number of instances, the founder was succeeded by family members for two or three generations. Eventually, however, it was necessary to look outside the family for operational leadership. In some situations, the family has retained the top post but operational control has become such a complex task that many of the most important operational decisions are made by executives who are not family members. When any of these circumstances occurred, the families in this study negotiated the transition from "rule to reign"—a process similar to that experienced by most successful modern monarchies.[2]

Distinguishing Between Managerial and Proprietary Interests

In the views of those who have gone through the transition to a professionally managed firm, or are in the process of doing so, it is critical to understand the difference between managerial and proprietary roles. One participant, the head of a Venezuelan insurance company, explained this distinction in a memorandum to company employees:

"A starting point had to be the members of my own family, who had not yet had the opportunity of becoming fully aware of their potential responsibilities as future shareholders. This involved their perception of what I consider to be an important feature of our capitalist society which, while upholding the principle of private ownership, also differentiates between ownership and the professional management needed to guarantee stability and continuity."

The "rule to reign" transition involves an informed acceptance by founders and their heirs of the separation of ownership from managerial concerns. Typically, it will have two distinct phases. In the first phase, founders identify and pursue those aspects of the business in which they are particularly skilled and interested. Other tasks, often including day-to-day operational control, are delegated to others.

Characteristically, the founder's interests run to developing new business opportunities, products or services. If, for example, it is a scientific or technological firm, founders may return to the laboratory. In companies where the founders' greatest creativity lies in the ability to devise complicated financial arrangements, they have often devoted their energies to acquisitions and divestitures. Successful transitions occur when founders go back to whatever activity was the real reason for their early success—and leave general operations, financial management, and legal issues to highly skilled professionals.

The second phase comes when the founder withdraws from day-to-day involvement and moves on to other pursuits. At this point, founders or their heirs become the *custodians of the firm's values* and the "reign and not rule" era really begins. This does not usually mean that the founder leaves the company altogether. Most founders retain a position on the board of directors, and continue to exercise control by reviewing important company decisions. The founder has a special interest in those activities that raise fundamental issues about the firm's basic mission. The most frequently cited examples of failures in the transition to institutionalization were situations where this oversight role was ignored—or badly played—by founders and their families.

Management Decisions and Fundamental Values

What are the management decisions that relate to these fundamental values? There was substantial agreement among study participants in all three geographic regions that they include the following:

Acquisitions and Divestitures

If a company began in the chemical business, the purchase of a food-processing company, however profitable, raises important questions. First, is the company going too far afield from its original mission? Will this imperil the quality of the core product—the goods or services that bear the company name? Second, will it radically alter the company culture and bring in a whole new group of employees that cannot be effectively integrated into the work force without a major change in the organization's values and rewards? Finally, will it alter the fragile balance between financial control and profitability that the family has set for itself? How important is equity control? Does the family want total control of a small company, or would it be happier with a smaller share of a larger, more profitable entity?

Many of these questions also arise in nonfamily firms. The difference is that the discussion may be more emotionally charged because it affects family members. In essence, they are being asked to build an addition to their home and to invite strangers to join them there.

Structure of Employee Relations and Selection of Top Managers

For those companies that put their basic principles in writing, a central issue is how employees are treated. Whether it is called "company culture," "morale" or the more institutional and impersonal term "employee relations," founders and their families usually have a basic credo that most believe has made a substantial contribution to their success. In their own view, they have created a company atmosphere that is pleasant and productive because each individual is treated with respect. The situation, in reality, may be different from this conception. Nonetheless, effec-

[2]The best-known example of "reigning" monarchs is, of course, the British royal "family firm." See, for example, Elizabeth Longford, *The Queen: Elizabeth II of England.* New York: Alfred A. Knopf, 1983.

tive successors understand that founders and their families expect them to operate within the framework of company tradition in their relations with employees. Although nonfamily-owned companies share many of these same concerns, the commitment to these practices in family firms often is strengthened by bonds of personal pride, loyalty and obligation.

As to management succession, the issue of the founder's replacement is of paramount concern to founders and their heirs. There is, of course, a pecuniary element: The family wants the company to continue making money. If the founder's successor demonstrates no talent for maintaining a profitable operation, the family is likely to want the individual replaced—with a fervor unmatched by less financially involved directors. But the more important issue for both employees and family is that a well-respected and often-beloved father figure is leaving. Will the new CEO inspire trust and confidence and show respect for the company's traditions? Many otherwise qualified executives have failed to live up to these demands, particularly with regard to preserving company traditions.

Management of Financial Resources

Many founders of businesses share similar attitudes toward their companies' financial resources. Founders of businesses in the United States, Latin America, and Europe generally express a preference for the internal financing of growth. As a result, they prefer not to pay dividends and they emphasize the reinvestment of profits in the company. They hope to use this strategy to retain control of the company and to increase their personal and family fortunes through stock appreciation. As for current income, as they can set their own salaries, there seems to be little sense in reducing the company's asset base through dividend payments.

The heirs tend to take a different point of view. Those who are employed by the company, or who have lucrative contractual arrangements with it, may continue to favor a non-dividend policy. But heirs who do not work in the company, and who have interests of their own to pursue, usually want their share of current profits. This is especially true where the heirs have shares tied up in trusts or other restrictive arrangements and cannot sell them. Whatever the case may be, both the founders and their families want to participate in decisions involving the financing of growth and the utilization of the company's financial resources.

Corporate Governance and Composition of the Board of Directors

It is through the board of directors that the family eventually implements the process of "reign and not rule"; the board is the company's ultimate guarantor of continuity. Among the companies interviewed were organizations where the family has not participated in day-to-day management for many years, but continues to dominate the board of directors. In two of these cases, the chairmen were family members (one of these had no business experience). While these situations are certainly examples of "reign and not rule," the principle is seldom effective when the family's representatives are not familiar with business and company practices.

Issues of Family Identity

Some eccentric, or personal issues, are unique to the particular company or individuals involved. Family members may choose to involve themselves in almost any decision. Even the building of a new company headquarters, or the selection of a logo for the company, can be seen by family members as interfering with the company's core identity and, hence, as grounds for direct involvement. No two companies or people are alike; but, as a rule, any management attempt to alter what the family believes to be the company's image will be resisted by family members.

Internal Mechanisms for Handling Failures and Misfits

A great many of the executives who were interviewed commented, either directly or indirectly, that their families were no more immune than any other to personal misfortune and to individuals who were not competent or suited to play a leading role in the business. All acknowledged the family's responsibility to care for "black sheep" and for those who had suffered personal catastrophes and were in need of financial assistance.

Problems arise when a family uses a company to satisfy these needs. Employment of an incompetent heir in a position of major operational responsibility not only impairs company performance, but it also erodes the legitimacy of family authority within the company. It fosters a climate of resentment among more capable family members who may feel that they should have a larger role to play. Although the principle is seldom stated explicitly, the families that report long-term and generally successful relations with their firms alluded to mechanisms, both formal and informal, for handling these kinds of problems.

It is evident that the transition process can be, and typically is, a painful one because of the emotional ties among those involved. It is a process of trial and error. Without a well-defined company mission and knowledgeable heirs who command respect and legitimacy (even though their experience and achievements may lie outside the company), the passage from "rule" to "reign" can be extremely hazardous. Still, all family companies that have survived for several generations have traveled this course successfully.

The underlying theme of all these basic principles is that they enable both the family and the business to be arenas of *personal growth and development* rather than arenas of *conflict*. They foster conditions that promote opportunity within the family and the business, and they establish mechanisms for the orderly resolution of conflict in both of these communities.

Chapter 3
Managing the Founder's Withdrawal

THE CRITICAL EVENT in the progression from founder-ascendant company to a business institution is the founder's withdrawal from active management of the firm. This was invariably a difficult period amoung participating companies, but it was especially traumatic if the company had failed to take the steps toward institutionalization which were described earlier.

The founder's departure is a test of how effectively the company's perception of its mission and its decision-making procedures enable founder, company and family to act in reasonable harmony. For each of these parties, the founder's disengagement necessitates a difficult adjustment to changed circumstances.

The founder will no longer be involved in day-to-day operations. Important decisions regarding the firm may now be made by former subordinates, some of whom may also be junior family members. A Latin American executive, commenting on the the difficulty of retiring after devoting most of his life to building a company, noted that the relationship he had with his company was one of deep attachment: "At first it is your mistress, but it winds up being your child." This metaphor has been used by others. However, those who have been through the process use it in discussion with considerable emotion.[1]

This suggests that the process of withdrawal from company leadership can be difficult for a founder. Evidently, the nature of this attachment changes and, as it does, the founder's emotional needs evolve from insistence on domination and control to a desire to give independence to a creation that will survive and serve as a monument.

The company's officers will be making and implementing key business decisions without the daily involvement of the founder. This will raise two questions in the minds of employees, customers, suppliers and the general public: *First,* has the organization gained sufficient credibility so that it can act in the absence of the founder's personal authority? Specifically, has the company's management-succession process achieved a stable transition and produced a leadership that can effectively represent the various elements within the company? Are business objectives clearly defined and consistent with the company's resources? Are policies and strategies in accord with the "company culture"? *Second,* are managers free to make important business decisions without fear of subsequent interference?

The family will confront one of two difficult situations: Either one of their number will be elevated to a position of primacy in the company, or the company will no longer be managed by a family member. In either event, the heirs will have to learn (if they have not done so already) how to exercise proprietary responsibilities. If someone from the family has become the company's operational head, other members will have to accept the individual's authority and acknowledge his or her ability to act as their representative.

* * *

In essence, this process raises two question about succession: (1) How can founders best manage their disengagement from the company; (2) How do founders delegate their personal authority? (With regard to the second issue, founders also observed that certain decisions are deemed nondelegable because they interfere with proprietary interests or, as is sometimes the case, only founders or their families command the personal authority to make them.) Thus, managing the founder's effective withdrawal from day-to-day company activity requires a delicate balancing act in the delegation of authority to a successor. It must be sufficient to allow them to act effectively as officers of the company but not so great as to interfere with the founder's proprietary concerns.

Why The Founder Retires

The threshold question for this discussion is: Why is the founder retiring? It follows that the individual's motive will influence the manner in which the disengagement process is handled.

---

[1]See Harry Levinson, "Conflicts that Plague Family Businesses." *Harvard Business Review, March-April, 1971.*

As a general proposition, founder-managers choose, or are compelled, to retire for one or more of the following reasons:

• *Personal:* This is the preferred motive because, except when occasioned by poor health, it is voluntary. The eventual persuit of personal goals—whether in the public arena of civic or cultural affairs, or in the more private cultivation of long-standing academic or recreational interests—is the stated desire of most founders of substantial business concerns. While these activities may prove less rewarding than anticipated, sometimes causing the founders to return to their involvement in their firms, the public and private accomplishments of individuals who have succeeded in these kinds of endeavors are well known.

• *Financial:* Other founders are less fortunate. Their companies fail to cope successfully with growing pains and, at some point, additional financing becomes necessary. The new investors want professional management and places for their representatives on the board of directors. One U.S. participant recalled: "As soon as we had to go to the bankers, things changed very quickly. They wanted five-year plans and projections. Every member of top management had to have substantial training and experience for us to get the investment community involved. There just did not seem to be a place in this new order for one of the founders." Nor is this problem uncommon. Another company—a Mexican manufacturer of office furniture—eventually found it necessary to retire two members of the founding family because of the demand for greater professionalism that resulted from the need for outside investors.

• *Organizational:* Participants noted that, ultimately, it is necessary to choose between lending aid and support to a new generation that, increasingly, is able to function on its own, or allowing the organization to atrophy by refusing to relinquish power in day-to-day decision making. It is at this point that the founder's most appropriate role becomes that of a wise counselor on questions of overall direction and policy.

Unfortunately, founders do not always know when to step down. French participants cited the example of a fabrics firm whose founder did an excellent job of building a business until he reached his sixties. He then hung on for nearly a quarter of a century, and thus destroyed the company.

"Life cycle" theorists have noted the difficulties that can occur when leaders hold on to their positions after age 65 or 70. Such individuals can become "out of phase" with their subordinates, who are impatient for opportunities of responsibility and leadership.

Indeed, even when the leader has the ability to continue, it may be advisable to step down to achieve an orderly transfer of power. Where this has not occurred, the founder can become isolated, lacking contact with associates and deeply resented by them. Relationships with managers who are in their forties can become fractious and hostile as these individuals, increasingly, feel that rightful authority is denied them. This poor morale can also affect younger members of the firm who are denied the active support that they, in turn, need from the middle generation.[2]

Sensing this, a Latin American business leader described the need for retirement at age 65 to his employees:

"Of course, good intentions are not enough. An explicit plan is required, with specific dates within which set objectives must be completed, clear pathways marked out, and full implementation warranted. Thinking that there will always be time to do these things is a way of shirking the heavy responsibility for carrying them out. Moreover, it must all be done in time, while the person in charge feels fully capable of monitoring a real transition, without being dangerously hasty. I feel this to be the position I am in."

Discussing Succession Within the Company

As they near retirement age, founders emphasize the need to provide for a stable succession and an orderly transfer of power that does not cause employee uncertainty about the future. The founder of a Latin American financial organization, in announcing his plans, noted that this was a major concern:

"I saw that we had to institutionalize our consortium, and maintain its independence from any individual person, so as to ensure the progress and careers of all those who constitute its large and extraordinary work force. It has always been our goal that the men and women who constitute that force should personally enjoy the security of knowing exactly where they stand, as well as the kind of future we can offer them."

His fellow participants in this study noted that the discussion of succession inside both family and company is a painful one. While succession may be a part of the founder's public agenda, the personal agenda may include a desire for ego gratification through the perpetuation of authority or the promotion of an unsuited, but favored, heir or employee to top operational responsibilities. Indeed, this individual went on to summarize these feelings in an unusually frank memorandum to the firm's employees:

"Naturally, the matter of who was to succeed me soon became a crucial point, as well as what such a transition would represent for me, for my family and, in general, for all the members of our organization. You must believe me that, in spite of understanding that all this just had to be done, it was a difficult, arduous and painful process. No one who feels fully alive and action oriented, who feels driven by the wish to create, serve and grow, feels quite happy to seriously discuss his own succession. Nevertheless, whoever

---

[2]For discussion of this point, see Daniel J. Levinson, *The Seasons of a Man's Life*. New York: Alfred J. Knopf, 1978, pp. 35-36.

refuses to face life's transitions easily may become their victim, or, even worse, may victimize those to whom he is committed."

Managing a Successful Departure

Those founders who have done it are agreed that retirement was one of the most challenging management tasks of their careers. In essence, it was a final judgment on how well they had constructed their businesses. The effort to build an edifice that could function without them started when the company was in its infancy and the various components that emerged were continually fine tuned. Those who had been successful, and respondents for companies that had achieved a fairly smooth transition from founder to successor at some point in the past, noted that certain factors were present in the founder's initial decision to retire:

• *First, the founder's retirement was timely*. A timely retirement is one that occurs while the founder is still in full command of his or her abilities, and is able to lend counsel to senior managers when it is sought. One of the most successful examples of such a retirement was found in a U.S. manufacturing firm in which the current CEO continued to consult with his predecessor on matters that the CEO deemed to be of vital importance to the firm.

Other departures were less timely—and less successful. The founder of a U.S. insurance company died suddenly and his post was filled by the Executive Vice President. The individual had never really been considered for the position by the founder, who had expected to be active for several more years. The new man was not well suited to the task and the company went into decline under his leadership. In another example, the head of a Mexican company departed abruptly to accept a diplomatic post. His two brothers did not prove to be effective replacements.

• *Second, the founder's retirement was unequivocal*. This does not mean that the individual ceases to play *any* role. That is rarely the case, and it is not considered desirable by those founders who have retired. "Unequivocal" suggests that the new role is well-defined and that it does not include participation in day-to-day business.

This is easy to state in principle, but hard to apply in practice. For example, although a Mexican entrepreneur announced his decision to retire from daily management activities, one of his top managers noted that it is still necessary to clear all important management decisions with the former boss. It appears that this retirement is causing some confusion among the company leadership and the effectiveness of his departure is questionable.

• *Third, the founder was publicly committed to an orderly succession plan*. Widespread awareness of the founder's imminent withdrawal and the specific changes in leadership that will result is deemed to be very important. One founder, for example, provided his employees with a three-year timetable that included a detailed description of phases of his successively reduced levels of participation.

• *Fourth, the founder has articulated and supervised the formulation of company principles regarding management accountability, policies, objectives and strategies*. If the company has not developed—or is not in the process of developing—a mission statement, it is critical that the effort be undertaken before the founder's departure. For these "credos" are the basis for continued guidance and control by founders and their families.

Among the companies participating in the study were organizations that did not succeed in this endeavor—and a few that did not even attempt it. However, participants point out that the success of the founder's partial or complete withdrawal from the scene is dependent, in large measure, on the extent to which basic principles of management accountability, business objectives, policies and strategies have been enunciated. Moreover, the mere promulgation of these guidelines is not enough. Some founders emphasized the value of participative processes over a long period of time in developing and refining these statements—primarily to avoid internal reaction that might otherwise be indifferent, sullen or even hostile. The founder of a South American company emphasized the importance of maintaining employee morale while this is happening: "We are in a service business. We don't have inventory, commodities, machinery; we just have people and their relationships both inside and outside the company. This is what I call 'connectional assets.' If you lose these people, or the relationships that the company has built up, you can lose just about everything."

One former CEO of a U.S. manufacturing company recalled that employee anxiety was very high when he undertook to formulate basic company principles for the first time: "It took us nine months to get the first draft on paper and during that time there was great impatience. We were dubbed 'the seven blocks of granite' by the middle managers because they had not seen anything come out of these talks.'"

Still, by common agreement, a nine-month process for this kind of exercise is not all that unusual. As explained by an heir who took over a U.S. manufacturing company:

"In 1962, when I became president, I realized almost immediately that the company was demoralized and living off the fruits of the past. A clear blueprint was needed if the company was going to maintain its independence. I needed to know how we could do this, what businesses we would be in, what would constitute satisfactory performance, and what strategies and values would help to accomplish our objectives.

"So I gathered together my team—six other guys who had marketing, manufacturing, engineering, finance, personnel and international backgrounds—and we sat down together and put one question up on the blackboard: *What kind of company do we want to be ten years from now?* We then embarked on a process that involved an assessment of our own personal values and goals, and of our long-term strengths, weaknesses, opportunities and threats.

"We decided that we did not want to be the biggest; we wanted to be the best. We did want to be a worldwide enterprise. We wanted the company to earn its independence. We wanted high performance in profitability and innovation. And we wanted to do this through internal development, rather than by buying an empire."

For this individual, the most serious complicating factor was that he and his colleagues also had to run the company while engaging in these deliberations, or, as he put it: "I felt as if I had one hand on the steering wheel and a copy of a Peter Drucker book in the other."

Statements of Principle: The Key Elements

Among those who have been through the process, there is substantial agreement that a company's formulation of its fundamental beliefs ought to contain an acknowledgment of management accountability to shareholders and a carefully detailed expression of company policy.

Management Accountability

Statements of management accountability and professionalism establish the company's public commitment to achieve status as a business institution. They tell the shareholders, employees, customers, suppliers—and the general public—that top management will be held accountable for both the company's results and for a high standard of professionalism. (See Exhibit 3.)

This is an important step for a family company to take because major shareholders who are also top managers could hold their positions indefinitely by virtue of their working control of the company. The implementation of these corporate principles entails the uncoupling of proprietary from managerial authority. One participant noted this distinction: "At least I could say that both my job and yours (the other employees) depends on our ability to satisfy the shareholders. It is the distinction between the boss functioning as a proprietor and the boss functioning as a hired hand, accountable to the shareholders."

This latter point—achieving legitimacy through competence, rather than ownership—was underscored by the founder of a U.S. manufacturing firm, who sold all but a small portion of his interest in the company and remained as CEO. His reason—"I wanted to provide security for my family and I felt that if the new shareholders did not want me to continue, I probably would not deserve the job anyway."

One Mexican company participating in this study went a step beyond management accountability principles and also formalized standards for professional managers. This suggests that the company will hold all managers accountable not just for results, but also for the manner in which they are achieved. (See Exhibit 4.)

Exhibit 3: A U.S. Manufacturer: Statement of Management Accountability

> ### Accountability of Yarway Management
>
> 1. We are accountable to our *customers* for satisfying their needs with products and services that give them optimum value in terms of performance and reliability.
> 2. We are accountable to our *employees* for providing opportunity, compensation, and supervision, in accordance with the basic policies in an environment where each person can find meaning and satisfaction in his work and where all employees recognize their common interest in the continuing achievement of corporate objectives.
> 3. We are accountable to our *stockholders* for achieving corporate objectives and for operating the company in accordance with the basic policies for Yarway Corporation.
> 4. We are accountable to our *suppliers* for representing our needs honestly, dealing with them ethically, and paying them promptly.
> 5. We are accountable to the *community* for operating a company that obeys the law, is a good neighbor, and supports worthwhile community undertakings.

Company employees value accountability standards because they want assurance that their efforts will be recognized and that they will not be abruptly replaced as heirs come of age. As one U.S. company president, who was not a family member, put it: "They're always waiting in the wings and everyone knows it."

Although well-defined standards of professionalism and accountability are designed to help dispel this kind of apprehension, they do not necessarily work that way—particularly among nonfamily members whose careers with the company date from the early stages of the business. These individuals may feel threatened by the adoption of impersonal standards that establish professional competence, rather than long-standing personal relationships, as the primary basis for evaluating performance. They may also have grown accustomed to operating by improvising and, as a result, may resent the additional burdens of planning and management that professional standards are likely to impose.

A somewhat typical example is the case of a U.S. insurance firm headed for the first time by a nonfamily member. This man had been the company's marketing executive and continued to focus on these activities after he became president. The company was publicly owned. When it grew to a certain size, the auditors started asking for sophisticated information systems. The president said he had done all that was necessary, but the accountants disagreed.

The board of directors grew uneasy with the company's lack of direction and asked for a strategic plan. It was never

Exhibit 4: Professional Standards: A Mexican Manufacturing Company

---

THE PROFESSIONAL MANAGER

The *professional manager* is a leader, a man of integrity, mature, motivated and capable of motivating; concerned with his own personal development and that of the persons collaborating with him.

He is capable of committing himself to the objectives he has to attain and to direct those under his command to perform the goals set.

He is capable of providing himself with self-control measures for his actions, to measure his own progress to make the necessary adjustments.

He is capable of adopting decisions and has an open mind to capture information and new ideas.

He is capable of organizing working relations, establishing the commitments and responsibilities of each unit under his area, presenting them always in terms of results.

He is capable of creating a pleasant working environment, based on principles expressed concretely in healthy policies to orientation; in an understanding toward and among persons, establishing interpersonal relations with principals, peers and subordinates, based in respect for the human being; in a participation that strives for the fulfillment of all the interested parties and in teamwork.

---

produced and the president continued to emphasize the valuable network of industry contacts that he had built up over the years. As one board member recalled: "We asked for a plan and got a set of off-the-wall projections about the company's future. He never really understood what kind of information systems the auditors wanted. It never occurred to the guy that he could learn on the job. He did not see it as a process of learning and adaptation. His strategy was to do what he had always done best. In the end, it did not work; there was no way that it could have worked."

Statements of Policy

Policy statements show how the organization's values and beliefs have been incorporated into the governance of the company. In this regard there are two major areas of concern: processes and growth. Exhibit 5 presents a comprehensive statement by a U.S. manufacturer.

Management Processes

Study participants consider a commitment to planning as a key element in the successful evolution of their firms. But, as some of the examples below illustrate, implementing a planning process where none has existed can give rise to serious antagonisms and anxieties among employees who have grown accustomed to successful company performance without it. Noting the importance of planning and the difficulty of implementing planning systems in his family's sugar company, a Belgian CEO observed that even the most elementary of planning exercises—budget discussions—called for careful management:

"Budgets are a good way to have a common language. A budget gives you the opportunity for the right kind of discussion. You can use it as a way of raising important issues or developing an approach to a problem. But you have to be careful; a budget discussion per se can cause a war."

Some companies encountered great difficulty in developing planning procedures. The heir and succesor to the founder of a garment-manufacturing firm recalled that this was a major cause of his eventual decision to sell the business:

"These people were used to short-term projects. It was hard to get them to think four or five seasons ahead. Because they were not used to the long view, they opposed every suggested plant expansion. They said it would be another mouth to feed—another factory that had to be kept fully operational. They did not see expansion as an opportunity for the future. In the meantime, they were under the gun to find a line that would keep the facilities that we had going."[3]

Another organization, a U.S. insurance company, never defined its core geographic markets or product lines because it did not have the institutional mechanisms to do so. When the founder died, he was succeeded by the underwriting and marketing specialist whose major objective was rapid growth. This was accomplished through expansion into regions and lines with which company employees had little experience. Moreover, the firm lacked the management processes that would facilitate an exchange of views and information. Although the company doubled in size in less than three years, thereafter it began to lose money. The president resigned and the directors chose as his successor an individual from outside the company who was determined to define a core mission for the organization as a regional company with significantly fewer product lines.

These illustrations point to several important factors:

(1) The hazards that can occur on the departure of a major player who has not considered the problems of people and institutional development are of particular importance in family businesses.

[3] For a discussion of operations managers and the planning discipline, see Rochelle O'Connor, *Preparing Managers for Planning*. The Conference Board, Report No. 781, 1980.

BASIC POLICIES

1. Human Values
The Company should be operated to enrich the lives of all people affected by it. Every effort should be made to respect the dignity and worth of all persons. Distinctions will not be made between people because of age, sex, race, religion or national origin.

2. Integrity
All personnel should maintain at all times the Company's tradition of integrity and high ethical and moral standards. This means conduct that is honest, lawful, consistent with recognized codes of business ethics, and free of conflict between personal interest and Company interest. It also means honestly representing Yarway products and services, avoiding disclosure of proprietary information and upholding Yarway's trade name and business reputation.

3. Opportunity
The Company should provide real opportunity for each employee to develop his highest potential, and to know the satisfaction of worthwhile accomplishment in a common undertaking. All employees should be encouraged to give responsible expression to their ideas, beliefs, and convictions with the objective of advancing knowledge and understanding.

4. Performance and Rewards
All positions in the Company should be staffed by employees who possess the personal qualities and the professional or trade qualifications required to achieve a high standard of performance in their work. The Company will expect better-than-average performance of its employees and will reward such performance with better-than-average compensation compared with other companies in the same labor market and industry. A suitable bonus plan or plans, based on profits, sales production or other measures of performance should be maintained to recognize and reward contributions to the Company's success made by employees individually and collectively.

5. Teamwork
Management should encourage cooperation and mutual assistance between individuals and groups throughout the Company. Problems should be faced promptly and squarely with emphasis on remedial and preventative action, rather than emphasis on past errors and omissions.

6. Supervision
Every employee who has responsibility for supervising the work of others should make sure that each of his subordinates understands clearly the results for which he is accountable. Furthermore, every supervisor should clearly establish each subordinate's freedom to act in achieving those results. Individuals and groups in the Company should participate whenever practical in making decisions which affect them or about which they have useful knowledge or competence. It is recognized that such participation does not alter the accountability for results of the responsible supervisor, although it can often improve the quality of his decisions, gain better acceptance of them, and provide growth opportunities for his subordinates.

7. Growth
The Company should grow according to plan. Growth should be in human relationships, creativeness, capability and productiveness, as well as in sales volume and profitability. Growth should be achieved primarily by means of internal development of products and markets and secondarily by acquisition of companies or products. The rate of growth should be no faster than can be staffed by well-qualified, properly oriented employees.

8. Company Objectives
Specific long-range Company objectives should be recommended by management and approved by the Board of Directors in the following areas:

- Profitability • Growth • Market Standing
- Products • Capability and Productiveness

These Company objectives, along with appropriate guidelines, should be incorporated in a Planning Guide for use by all members of management. They should be reviewed annually by management and the Board of Directors to keep them relevant to changing conditions.

9. Planning
Management is expected to take a long-range point of view in all of its planning. Each year management should prepare detailed budgets for the next two years and a forecast of orders by product line for each of the next five years. The budgets should include shipments and gross profit for each product line, profit and loss statements, balance sheets, and major capital expenditures. Budget preparation should be intimately related to development of marketing plans, product plans, organization development plans, and financial plans.

10. Military Business
Planned Company growth should not be made dependent upon military markets.

11. Products
There should be continued development of new and improved products which meet the following conditions:
a. New products should fulfill customer needs in a new and better way and serve worthwhile purposes.
b. New products should be selected to capitalize on the knowledge and resources of the Company.
c. New product development should be directed solely toward industrial and commercial rather than military markets.
d. New product development should be undertaken only when sound market research promises steady, profitable sales volume.

12. Product Reliability
Yarway products should be designed, manufactured and sold to the high standards that will provide the user with dependable value in terms of performance and reliability.

13. Accounting Practices
Conservative accounting practices should be followed. The maximum allowable write-off should be taken as a charge against current operations for obsolete or slow-moving inventory, depreciation, development expense, maintenance expense, and other such items. Adequate provision should be made for funding pension commitments. All accounts will be audited regularly by a certified public accountant selected by the Board of Directors.

14. Contributions
Contributions of 1% to 3% of pre-tax profit should be made each year to support charitable, educational and community activities, either directly or through the medium of the Yarway Foundation.

15. Dividend Policy
Total dividends on all classes of stock should average 4% to 5% of net worth.

(2) The planning process plays an important role in management training and development. Establishing business objectives through cooperative endeavor helps to identify those individuals who work well as part of the team effort, and who are also effective in achieving the company's stated goals.

(3) Growth is dangerous if not accompanied by institutional sophistication and changes in management processes.

(4) Key employees can retain their leadership roles only to the extent that they recognize the need for personal growth and adaptation.

If establishing formal processes where none have existed presents difficulties, the reverse can also be true. Over a period of time, many family companies establish a form of feudalism in which personal loyalties are often emphasized at the expense of initiative and aggressiveness. The head of a Belgian sugar company found it necessary to break down the excessively formal practices that threatened the firm's future. He described the changes that he made to motivate employees:

"Our people are now allowed to function independently and they are promoted fast. They become a success story and this makes it easier for us to get better people. We are spending more for motivation. We are trying to give maximum power to our managers.

"We use small teams followed by a good control system. We promote them on competence, efficiency, drive and risk taking. This was not done in the past when consistency and devotion to the company were the most important criteria for advancement. People who rocked the boat were quarantined. We are looking for a very different profile. This shocks the older generation very much.

"Before all this started, the company had a different culture. You were over fifty before you reached the managerial level. Everything was formal and conventional. We are trying to have a new breed of managers. We want a highly decentralized operation with managers who can handle independence."

The informality of some family companies can be intriguing and attractive—sometimes to great advantage. Explaining why he switched to a family-owned company, its current CEO says:

"I wanted very much to get into the personnel field. I had been with a large company for eight years and there were still thirteen people ahead of me in a personnel department of more than two hundred people. I was on vacation and I saw this classified ad, written in an extremely intriguing manner, and I responded to it. It attracted me because of the way it described what would be expected of the person and what it said about the company's philosophy. I wanted to send them a resume, but all I had was a piece of white note paper from the place where I was staying. So I just jotted down one-liners about the salient factors in my background and sent it in."

The emphasis on unique opportunities and the effort to attract high-quality professional managers is not without risk to a family company because the primary loyalty of professionals may be to their own careers. In the view of a Belgian executive, losing someone for that reason can actually be an occasion for some satisfaction:

"For the first time we had a young man who left us for a major management position with a large company. To me this was a good sign; we now have people who can make the grade with major U.S. companies. In the past, an American company would never have accepted one of our people. For the first time, a good manager left us. And maybe one day we will go after him because the experience that he will get there could be precious to us."

What emerges from these recollections of major effort by family concerns to institute management accountability, professional standards, planning procedures, company business goals, and career objectives for long-term employees is that they arise in, or precipitate, an "organizational crisis." For employees, this "crisis," like the Chinese pictograph for the word, may hold the prospect for either danger or opportunity.

Sometimes a family company lacks the leadership or consensus to make necessary changes. Participants from two companies noted that consultants can be helpful in these circumstances. One observed:

"Our board had no leadership and it could not agree on what needed to be done. A consulting group was retained to investigate the company's practices and procedures. When they delivered their report, the board members said it had not told them anything that they did not already know. What they failed to realize was that these appraisals do not provide people with new information. They exist to confirm suspicions, to give people impartial verification of what they already know, to promote greater confidence in their own opinions among managers and directors, and, ultimately, to build a consensus for specific action. Obviously, the consultants were useful in this regard."

Achieving Growth

Among those founders who were interviewed, there was substantial emphasis on the importance of achieving growth and profits *in a manner consistent with maintaining their own, and the company's independence.* This concern is evident in their professed commitment to the following policies:

— *Quality products or services that help the company to establish a high status and an independent reputation.* More than one participant echoed the view of the individual who said: "We do not want to be the biggest; we want to be the best."

In practice, what sort of decisions does this mean? First, there is emphasis on prestige products, long-term business relationships, and a highly regarded position in the market which they compete. Having their name on the door leads families to emphasize these priorities within their companies and it puts a brake on opportunistic approaches to business and planning decisions. Consistent with this view, family companies utilize strategeis that often rely heavily on the development of "in-house" capabilities.

— *Avoidance of undue reliance on a single product or customer.* Substantial dependence on a particular business relationship can be dangerous if for any reason, the arrangement turns sour. Founders were also concerned that the other party might make unreasonable demands on the company and jeopardize the firm's independence.

This point is illustrated by a story involving Adolph Ochs, the owner of the *New York Times.* In the days when the paper's financial resources were extremely limited, Ochs refused an offer from a friend for $150,000 worth of municipal advertising with "no strings attached." He made his decision on the theory that he needed the revenue so desperately that he might adjust his operation to the windfall. He was unwilling to trust himself if he was threatened with a cancellation of the contract after that happened.[4]

— *Conservative dividend policy.* Emphasis on internally financed growth generally results in a conservative dividend policy for family companies. As has already been noted, founders prefer reinvestment of profits to paying dividends. The heir to, and now CEO of, a Belgian company stressed that the founder's personal, as well as business philosophy, can be a factor: "My father never paid a dividend because he wanted us to learn to live prudently and independently."

The issue of dividend policy can be hotly debated when stewardship of the firm passes to subsequent generations (see page 22). At this later point, the family may look to the company to satisfy a proliferation of interests.

Involvement versus Delegation: The Founder's Dilemma

In many instances, it is difficult to reconcile the founder's intense involvement in all aspects of the business with the need to delegate authority that is essential for building a successful institution. When founders do preside over the company's evolution to a business institution, it is largely because they have been adaptable enough to change their own role as the company evolved to institutional maturity.

Steinberg Inc., the subject of an extensive study began as a small grocery store in Montreal, Canada, in the early part of the century.[5] Sam Steinberg, at age 13, believed that his family could successfully operate additional stores. The young man displayed a genius for selecting successful locations and went on to master all facets of the business. He

was knowledgeable about the quality of the produce he sold and the suppliers who provided it. He recruited effective personnel and knew how to control costs. He built a strong coalition of suppliers, customers and employees who responded to his leadership. His self-assurance comes through in his reflections on the reasons for the company's success: "I knew merchandise, I knew cost, I knew selling, I knew customers, I knew everything. . .and I passed on all my knowledge; I kept teaching my people. That's the advantage we had. They couldn't touch us." His near obsession with details was matched by his emphasis on teaching.

Successful institutionalizers are dedicated teachers. Companies that enjoy the least hazardous transition to independent institutions almost invariably have founders who realize and act on the perception that the firm exists to promote certain values and to transfer necessary skills to employees so that, ultimately, they can function independently in a manner consistent with these basic principles.

This company eventually became one of the largest merchandising concerns in Canada. But it has not strayed far from the founder's original outlook of how the business ought to be run. In this connection, Mintzberg and Waters noted that Steinberg and many key managers in the firm could get as involved in the question of the quality of a shipment of strawberries as in the decision to open a chain of restaurants.

Involvement in this kind of day-to-day issue is, perhaps, the single most important characteristic of those interviewed for this study. To cite another example, a biographer of Charles Revson related that the founder of Revlon would test the company's nail polish by putting it on his own fingernails, a skill he had learned for demonstration purposes. "To this day, I try colors on myself. What you gotta learn, you gotta learn."[6]

Both of these examples depict in vivid terms a founder's preoccupation with all details of the business. The difference between these two men, however, was Sam Steinberg's belief in the importance of "teaching his people." In contrast, Charles Revson's lack of interest in the mentor's role is well known. Although both Steinberg Inc. and Revlon are highly successful companies, Revlon had difficulty attracting and keeping top managers and was not entirely successful in institutionalizing its management processes until after Revson's death.

Ensuring Continuity: The Role of the Board of Directors

A founder who has effected a smooth transition establishes institutional mechanisms that resemble those of a constitutional government. The statement of basic principles serves as a constitution and the company's management systems function legislatively to amend or modify these views in light of the company's developing experience and its current

---

[4]Gay Talese, *The Power and the Glory.* New York: Bantam Books, 1970, 15.

[5]Harry Mintzberg and James A. Waters, "Tracking Strategy in the Entrepreneurial Firm." *Academy of Management Journal,* Vol. 25, No. 3, 1982.

[6]Andrew Tobias, *Fire and Ice.* New York: Warner Books, 1977, p. 54.

Within this framework, the board of directors provide[s] assurance that the company's most important determination[s] will be consistent with its long-run objectives and will n[ot] violate the rights of individual shareholders. In a fami[ly] enterprise, the board plays certain roles:

It supervises the company's development of institution[al] sophistication;

It assists the founder, company and family in adjusti[ng] to the founder's disengagement from active management [of] the firm;

It serves as an agent of family control after the found[er] retires from day-to-day management activities.

In the early stages—when growth is imperative—ma[ny] founders defer these *managerial* and *institutional* concer[ns] in favor of more immediate business considerations: (1) T[he] board is a legal necessity; (2) coalition members want to pa[r]ticipate in board deliberations; and (3) founders need t[he] support of this group for their programs.

When growth is achieved and the company becomes [a] public institution, the board's institutional role as represe[n]tatives of the interests of the shareholders and the pub[lic] becomes critical. Indeed, in extremely large publicly owne[d] companies, it is the practice (in some cases, the necessit[y]) to add "public members," who represent the large interes[ts] of society. Some European codetermination laws also requi[re] employee representation on the board.

A changing approach to the choice of members reflec[ts] the board's role at various junctures in the company['s] history. In the *coalition* phase, the board exists primarily [to] support the founder's initiatives and it is largely compose[d] of the individuals who were brought together to build t[he] company. At the *founder-ascendant* stage, the board's ro[le] is to oversee the functional management of the compan[y]. Once the company has evolved into a *business institutio[n]*, the board is expected to act to protect the interests of all t[he] shareholders and the public.

Few would disagree with this conceptual model. Proble[ms] arise in its implementation by family companies. Becau[se] the power to choose directors often remains the exclusi[ve] perquisite of founders or their families, a founder or he[ir] may be faced with the unpleasant task of telling lifelo[ng] friends or trusted and valued employees that their servic[es] on the board are no longer desirable. In some instances, [it] may also be necessary to ask key suppliers to resign becau[se] closer public scrutiny of the company's business relatio[n]ships makes the individual vulnerable to conflict-of-intere[st] charges.

There are additional reasons why founders are not alwa[ys] inclined to seek able directors once it becomes essential [to] do so. It reminds them of their own mortality. And eve[n] if recruitment of board members is a high priority from t[he] outset, a fledgeling company may not be able to attract i[n]dividuals who can make a major contribution to a high-ris[k] low-paying directorship. In time, these directorships w[ill] become more prestigious. But the need for a board with[...]

human and financial resources. Management processes are also a key element in the selection of a new generation of leadership and in the choice of, and the orderly transfer of power to, a new CEO. But effective management systems do more than produce decisions—they also *legitimize* them. The process of debate and discussion that they require secures commitments from the parties to accept and to implement major company initiatives.

Becoming a Business Institution: A Mexican Perspective

The Mexican businessmen interviewed differ from the U.S. and European respondents in their analysis of problems associated with the successful institutionalization of management processes. This view is the product of different cultural and economic circumstances, of which the following were considered the most important.

First, Latin American families are more likely to involve their children in the business and to think that it is desirable to do so. What might be considered nepotism in the United States is often seen as preparation for, and acceptance of, a necessary role that heirs must play in the promotion of the family's destiny within the community.

Second, the lesser amount of capital available for investment in private enterprise has produced a situation in which fewer Latin American companies have the participation, oversight and interference of nonfamily members in company business activities. In this connection, many people complained that the high rate of interest paid on government obligations also contributed to the shortage of capital available for private enterprise. As a consequence, many families often do not have the option of reducing their level of involvement or of selling their companies.

The stronger bonds between family and business that arise from cultural values and economic circumstances lead to different, rather than fewer, problems. In a wide-ranging discussion, a prominent lawyer, who received his professional degree in the United States, summarized the difficulties faced by family firms:

"From my experience, it is much easier to make the transition from a family-owned business to professional management in the United States. This is a by-product, in part, of temperament. In many respects, as individuals, we are much more domineering than Anglo-Saxons. Then, while we have excellent and outstanding managers in Mexico, management is a new science in many ways. As your economy is much stronger than ours, the need for professional managers has existed for a longer time. In Mexico, it is a much more recent trend—going back no more than 30 years. I do not think that Mexicans or, for that matter, any Latins, are inclined to accept professional management."

In its extreme, the mentality described may lead to a counterproductive emphasis on ownership and control over profits. In that regard, he recalled a recent experience:

"A friend of mine owns a business that is worth—to pick a figure—$3 million. He would rather own 100 percent of that business than 80 percent of a $5-million business. This happens all the time. When I was with a law firm, we were once discussing whether or not to readmit someone who had left the firm. Many of the partners argued against it because it would mean a lower percentage of the profits for them. I thought that was absurd; they really did not understand that he might bring in more money and make them richer."

Lack of a diverse group of shareholders has an effect on institutionalization because it makes the company's effort to find qualified managers more difficult. He noted that this can also be a problem:

"I would say that individuals with industrial management or business education would rather go into a company that is not family owned. If someone works for a publicly held company, he is likely to feel more secure in his job. If the president is not the founder-owner, but just another professional manager, he is more likely be objective in judging individual performance. You can also disagree with the number-one man more easily."

A further problem noted by this attorney was the government's frequent insistence on local equity control of joint ventures because this requirement is an indirect limitation on the growth of a pool of professional managers. Many observers believe that an influx of foreign capital might transfer skills to the host country and help Mexico to develop its infrastructure:

"Foreign companies operate under serious limitations. Depending on the situation, they have to allow various percentages of the venture to be locally owned. There might be a shortage of risk capital anyway and these factors increase the problem. Then the government comes in and sets all sorts of restrictions on the use of technology. A lot of foreign companies look at this situation and decide not to go into Mexico. When they do not come, the opportunities for a lot of people to develop professional skills are lost."

One of the more important effects of Mexico's roller-coaster economy is a great concern among business leaders with the shortage of talent and the lack of a stable employment environment that they believe is critical for developing managerial competence. Indeed, Mexican owners were much more likely to emphasize problems in recruitment and training than were their American and European counterparts.

All of those interviewed complained of difficulty in finding and keeping qualified professionals during the boom years in the late 1970's. Finding people is the obvious problem, but keeping them may be more serious in the long run. When managers change jobs often there are fewer opportunities for the long-range enhancement of skills. With the constant shifting and changing of personnel, the long-term relationships between jobs and people—an essential component of institutionalization—are harder to establish.

Because highly qualified professionals are more likely to leave their posts for positions elsewhere, and the discipline imposed by a shareholding public is seldom present, the pressure for institutionalization of the business, in many instances, comes from the family rather than from professional managers or nonfamily shareholders. Among the Mexican companies studied, the transition from a founder-ascendant firm to an institution has generally been the result of negotiation *within* the family rather than the consequence of arrangements worked out *between* the family and the company, as is often the case in the United States.

The company's role in the transfer of skills and the sharing of experience is especially significant in Latin America. In the United States and Europe, the much larger number of business-training courses and opportunities to gain experience allow both family and employees to be less dependent on their own company to perform this function. Inasmuch as Latin American firms are also more likely to have a greater number of family members in important positions in the company, family relationships are also employment relationships. The result is a greater dependence on one another for mastering the skills of the business and for gaining the experience that will enable one generation to succeed another in leading the organization.

wider range of talents and experiences will also become more urgent.

Nonetheless, there may be a natural loyalty to those who were willing to serve the company in its earlier days when the risks were great and the rewards were few. Because of this appreciation for earlier allegiance, founders and families do not always exhibit the same ardor to replace a board member who is no longer adequate (particularly when the person gives them unqualified support) as they show toward long-term managers who have lost their talent for making profits.

A further consideration in perpetuating the tenure of weak directors is the founder's control of all (or a substantial portion of) the shares in the company. In an atmosphere where public attention is lacking, some founders view a feeble board, dependent on them and totally responsive to their wishes, as being very much in their own interest.

Thus, the attitude of founders and their heirs will determine, in large measure, whether the board is an agent of, or barrier to, change. Some boards promote institutional sophistication and function as a major catalytic agent in the company's progress toward this objective. In other cases, the board lags behind, and the company's developing needs provide the impetus for the next phase of development.

Examples of both situations were found among the study participants. Two CEO's commented that they considered the board of directors to be an especially important resource. They wanted the services of individuals who had the stature and the self-confidence to disagree with them. As a Belgian CEO put it: "The chairman is much more than an ordinary chairman. He is my last resort. He is not a member of the family. I would like to have more people like him and have committees on auditing and on strategic issues."

A U.S. CEO made a similar observation: "Sometimes I have argued in favor of a proposition that I believed in, but the board has turned me down. Driving home from a meetin[g] like that, I have asked myself why I put up with all this; [it] is my company. Then I realize that this is why one has [a] board—to tell you when you might be wrong. If not for peo[p]ple who can disagree, the board would not be giving yo[u] needed help."

In one case, the founder and his heirs neglected the com[pany's] institutional needs in the selection of directors. A[n] heir recalled the problems that resulted:

"We did not have the kind of board you need when a com[pany] gets into trouble. The firm had grown rapidly in siz[e] and in the complexity of its operations, but there had bee[n] no change in the board of directors in six years. It consiste[d] of outside directors with no industry experience—wh[o] thought that their primary role was to offer the CEO un[e]quivocal support—and employees who felt that they had litt[le] choice in the matter. There was no one who had the ex[]perience to realize that the company was not growing in [a] healthy way. Finally, we replaced two of the employees wit[h] a couple of high-powered people who had good credential[s].

"The day finally came when the board recognized i[ts] responsibility to the shareholders and demanded the pres[i]dent's resignation. A major factor that influenced two [of] the directors was that key employees had said, in so ma[ny] words, that this would be desirable. Even at that point, th[e] directors had problems with the situation. They insisted o[n] going around the table and each one told the president wh[y] this had to be done.

"Unfortunately the other directors viewed the board [as] an extension of the company and the CEO as a fello[w] employee. While I looked at the whole thing the way [a] political rival does when his opponent is forced out after [a] period of ineptitude, each of these guys felt like someon[e] who has to fire a colleague after 20 years of service."

Chapter 4

Family's Preparation for the Founder's Retirement

DISENGAGEMENT OF THE FOUNDER from active management raises special considerations for the family. A number of participants observed that if the family does not plan for the founder's retirement, there can be unfortunate consequences.

There is no widespread agreement among families as to the best way to handle this situation. Companies can adhere to procedures and management techniques that are generally applicable for firms that are changing their leadership. This alone can establish a good deal of the foundation needed for a stable transfer of authority. Families do not have this frame of reference. Even if they can share experiences (and there is a growing tendency to do so), each family's efforts in this regard are subject to unique requirements. In addition, psychological or interpersonal reasons may render this process unsatisfactory—or worse, cause it to be deferred, thereby resulting in a change in company leadership without prior family discussion or preparation.

What emerges in these interviews with founders and their families is less of a prescription for a successful transition than it is an analytic framework for appropriate preparation. Families, unlike companies, have fewer widely accepted solutions available to them in making a successful transition because they consider themselves to be unique. There is, however, substantial agreement on the questions that arise in family discussions. These are: (1) Who is a member of the family for the purposes of stewardship of the company? (2) what is the appropriate process for determining the role that each family member will play in the company? (3) What company roles are available to individual family members? (4) What are the likely career and economic interests of each role category? (5) Is there a possibility of generational or cultural conflict within the family or between family members and career employees? If so, can it be avoided?

Who Is a Family Member

In the context of a family business, those who are family members may be different from those who are part of the family in the domestic sense. Certain children, for example, may be excluded from this group for business purposes. Similarly, a founder's spouse, if not active in the business, may not be part of the inner circle's deliberations on family business affairs. Husbands and wives of children may or may not be involved, depending on personal qualities or family sensitivities. Aside from the question of their moral claim to the founder's patrimony, the possibility of divorce makes families reluctant to share their secrets with a potential, or even possible, defector from its ranks. In addition to those with ties of blood or marriage to the founder's family, there are also individuals who inherit privileged relationships to companies by virtue of their membership in families of early backers, employees, customers and suppliers.

For the family businesses participating in this survey, there is a clear trend toward more family involvement in business issues and a greater utilization of the resources that the family can provide. This was observed in the United States, Latin America, and Europe.

Among the European participants interviewed, for example, it was fairly common practice for families to discuss their interests at annual meetings, which are similar to those convened for shareholders. Written financial data are distributed and company officers give reports. The family may also consider other issues that are pertinent to its financial health and stability, such as the special needs of certain members. Similar gatherings also occur in Latin America, but no American participant alluded to this kind of meeting. Quite possibly, U.S. families use foundations as a vehicle to serve at least one of these objectives—the extended discussion of the family's role in the community at large.

Families are no less impervious to change than other institutions. Discussions with participants reveal a clear trend toward greater equality for female heirs. In all three regions, there are many family businesses in which daughters have worked for the company in some capacity and are being prepared for important operational or oversight responsibilities. Although this appears to be consistently true, it is also evident that male heirs continue to be favored.

Companies also utilize the spouses of children in the leadership of the firm. Quite possibly this is because, by and large, fortune has favored companies that have relied on the talents of able sons-in-law. Indeed, one of the largest and oldest of the surveyed companies owed its survival to the efforts of such individuals early in its history.

The prevalence of divorce in contemporary life has added risks for families that take this course. In one of the companies surveyed, for example, the most capable potential successor among third-generation family members is separated from his wife (the daughter of the current CEO). The professional relationship of the two men has not, thus far, been materially affected by this development. However, the CEO is concerned as to whether the residual strain and bitterness will not eliminate this candidate from contention as his successor.

Choosing the Proper Role in the Business for Family Members: A Planning Process

Families are beginning to develop formal procedures for determining the distinctive competencies of each individual member, and the group as a whole, with regard to the businesses that they own or control. Although this approach is relatively new, there is growing interest in the utilization of processes and expertise that will enable families to participate in a meaningful and positive way in the institutional evolution of their companies. This amounts to a strategic-planning process designed to take cognizance of the requirements of family life.

One family undertook this effort in a highly formalized and structured way. The program that it described has been used by a number of Latin American and Canadian families. The exercise is conducted under the supervision of a well-known business consultant and his wife, who is a psychotherapist. A participant described how it worked:

"We began a process whereby we would meet as a family three or four times during the course of a year. These meetings would last a whole weekend. We started out with my father sharing his concerns about both the family and the firm. The consultants were drawn in and each made contributions from his or her perspective."

The participants were also encouraged to discuss the feelings toward and relationships with one another that might impede the achievement of the founder's goals. The therapist guided the discussion into sensitive areas and probed beneath the surface of emotions and attitudes. Both the father and the son agreed that these sessions were difficult experiences for all concerned. But they also felt that they were necessary if each participant was to arrive at an understanding of the role that he or she would play in the transition process. Once this was done, the family was ready for the second step, which was a series of presentations designed to give them a better understanding of the business. A family memb[er] recalls this part of the process:

"This started a series of discussions through which t[he] family was educated about the business. For us, the distin[c]tion between business and ownership interests was the ke[y.] So these discussions provided training on both business a[nd] ownership problems for everyone but my brother, who [was] involved in the business. The rest of us knew very little abo[ut] it."

The brother and important employees gave brief lectur[es] on the technical aspects of the industry in which the com[any] pany was involved. One brother-in-law, a stockbroker, ga[ve] a presentation on accounting and finance principles whi[ch] was helpful to the family in gaining an economic understan[d]ing of how the company worked. Top managers provide[d] further perspectives on "why the company was in a particula[r] business, and the importance of that business for the larg[er] system." And a consultant discussed "strategic issues a[nd] the difference between owning a company and managing it[.]"

Contact with top executives had an important effect [on] the family: "We learned that these people really did exis[t] and that they are very sharp. It brought home to us that [if] these people were to walk out, the family's future would [be] severely threatened."

It also helped the family to understand the role that ea[ch] individual member could play. One of the brothers was i[n]volved in the business and knew the fundamentals of the i[n]dustry. The brother-in-law who was a stockbroker ha[d] expertise in financial and economic analysis. And one so[n] who had pursued a career that at first appeared to [be] unrelated to the business, found he could also make a co[n]tribution:

"Given my professional background in psychology I w[as] better able to understand some of the struggles that my fath[er] was going through, and some of the problems that I and t[he] rest of the family had as we began to deal with issues su[ch] as death. This is a hot potato in any family. We tried to ma[p] out its repercussions for the family system.

"In terms of the succession issue vis-a-vis the family, [I] think my role is clearer to me. I feel that I can play a ro[le] as mediator. I am entitled to play that role because I ha[ve] skills to bring the family together on issues that they mig[ht] use just to hit each other over the head with."

But, as this individual concluded, "hitting each other ov[er] the head" is less likely now that this intensive exercise ha[s] been completed:

"The process of involving the family had very positive si[de] effects. For the first time we had an opportunity to lea[rn] about each other as adults. This is hard to come by in mode[rn] families because you are scattered all over the place. In ad[d]dition, it made us confront fundamental issues like parent[al] death. We realize that we either sink or swim together.

as taken three years, and there has been considerable in-
olvement.''

This kind of searching inquiry has been undertaken by
number of Latin American and Canadian families that
ave participated in the same program. Overall, however,
he approach is not widespread. Still, it is a formal descrip-
ion of a process that all families go through in one way or
nother.

Families that achieve a successful transition from founder
o professional management have found some way of iden-
ifying and capitalizing on the appropriate contribution that
ach family member can make. In this way, families can
ake use of valuable resources that no competitor may be
ble, or inclined, to use.

One family, for example, is represented on its company
oard by a world-famous academic whose expertise has, in
he view of its chairman, proven to be invaluable to the firm.
lthough he has a distinguished reputation in his field, the
ndividual probably would not be considered for a director-
hip of a company of comparable size in that particular in-
ustry.

When There Is No Planning

When the dynamics of the situation do not permit the kind
f careful planning described above, resolution is achieved
ore as a result of manipulation than as the end product
f careful analysis.

A fifty-year-old Mexican manufacturing firm overcame
otential family resistance to taking the necessary transitional
eps. The founder had three sons who were active in the
usiness. One of the sons was clearly the leader. When he
eft to accept a political appointment, the family had to find
way to upgrade its top management. They decided to sell
0 percent of the company to a group of investors in an ef-
ort to "institutionalize" the company. A third-generation
amily member explained the approach:

"By institutionalizing the company, I mean trying to make
he company into a public corporation. We wanted to get
ome resources from the stock market to finance new pro-
ects to expand the company. We had not had any in-
estments in product development or in diversification since
945.''

Although the sale was not part of a conscious effort to
ase the two remaining brothers out of management posi-
ons (it did, after all, have their approval), this was the
ltimate effect:

"I don't think that there was any other way to do it in
close family. We might have taken the family members
ut of management and given them positions on the board.
ut this would have been difficult because they had been
nvolved in the company for the last thirty years.

"So the first step was to sell part of the company and add
eople to the board who could manage it. The second step

was for certain family members to retire from day-to-day
operations. We are now involved in the third step—hiring
professional people to manage the company. If there are
family members who can do the job, they will have the same
chance as anyone else.''

Obviously, public ownership can be a vehicle for getting
family members to retire from key posts. In this case it was
used *by the family*, rather than by employees and other major shareholders, to get the individuals to withdraw. But profitable operations clearly eased a painful transition. Because
the company had substantial earnings during this period, the
family was able to find the means to compensate the depart-
ing members in ways that made retirement attractive.

Family Members: Roles and Interests

Whether the process is open and formal, as described
earlier in this section, or indirect and largely the product of
circumstance, as is more often the case, families eventually
determine the role that each individual member will play in
the evolution of the business. This role-selection process is
both a family and a business necessity. Within the family,
for example, children are not involved in the company's
decision-making process or in its institutional development.
However, when these children become adults with personal
ambitions and abilities, and a sizable stake in the company
that they either own or will some day inherit, it becomes appropriate to determine the role for which each individual is
best suited.

This, in turn, can create further tensions because the interests that are consistent with a particular role are not always
compatible with the concerns of other family members who
have taken a different part. Recognition of this fact, and
the establishment of an ongoing process for the discussion
and mediation of these conflicting views, can be of great
benefit to both the family and the company. In those instances where families have failed to resolve disputes within
their own ranks, the debate has often been carried on, at
great cost, within the company.

Participants identified three roles that individual family
members can play in the company—owner, overseer or
operator. Each of these has its own particular set of obligations, interests and concerns:

• *Owners are individuals who* are shareholders in a company in which their family has a substantial ownership position. Owners are, typically, better informed on company and
industry issues than are ordinary stockholders. This expertise includes knowledge of the identity, positions and historic
roles of key shareholders. With regard to the company,
familiarity with the industry or industries in which it is active, and the company's fundamental outlook toward
employees and the community are viewed as important. This
group, in most instances, also develops a common position
as a to the family's level of commitment to the company.
(For example, can or should individual members sell company stock?)

Of all the different role categories, owners tend to be the least patient with poor company performance. Their public identification with the firm, and contact with its leadership—particularly after the founder retires—is often minimal. They can therefore, be expected to seek a maximum overall rate of return on their asset.

• *Overseers are individuals who* are, or will become, directors. In this capacity, they will perpetuate the family's control and represent it on the board. Accomplishing these ends generally requires a grasp of all the essential ownership principles stated above. In addition, founders tend to involve them sufficiently in the activities of the company so that they can be well acquainted with key managers and directors. In order to promote the family's interests within the company effectively, overseers are also helped by an understanding of board practices and traditions. This will provide political insight into how important players can be persuaded and motivated to support family initiatives.

The patience of overseers with the performance of a company's top managers is often greater than that of the owners, but is typically less than that of the third group—the operators. The primary legal and moral responsibilities of overseers are to their fellow shareholders and not to the company's managers. Their distance from day-to-day involvement with the firm's executives and their lack of income from the company (other than director's fees) also help to lend a more objective air to their assessment of its performance.

• *Operators are individuals who* are able and willing to assume managerial posts. In addition to the understanding developed by the first two groups of family members, industry experience and knowledge of day-to-day company operations are essential for operators. As noted earlier, many founders consider it desirable for heirs to have important achievements and experiences outside the company so as to confer legitimacy and develop self-confidence. It is also viewed as helpful for the individual to have an in-depth knowledge of the company before assuming major operational responsibilities. This is often gained under the tutelage of the founder or a trusted employee.

Those family members who enjoy a financially remunerative relationship with the company, such as lawyers, consultants, accountants or suppliers, are also part of this operator group. This particular segment of the family is likely to show greater willingness to defer short-term gains in favor of long-run prospects for two reasons: First, they share the same concerns as the company's management and they have a community of interest with them. Second, up to a point, their impatience is assuaged by the salaries or fees that they derive from the firm despite its poor performance.

Selecting Family Members for Management Positions

Those families whose members are successful as top managers of the family's company tend to set high standards of training and experience (both inside and outside the firm) for heirs who seek a management role inside the company.

Sometimes, however, the family's standards are so strict that they virtually preclude involvement of some members.

For example, one executive of a Belgian company commented flatly: "It was laid down by the founder that no family member could work for the company unless he or she really stood a chance to become a partner." Moreover, there seemed to be no question of the family's ability to select its own business leaders at an early age.

In other cases, the family hesitates to expose its own members to the kind of personal risks that are essential to building a successful career. A British heir observed that the family's caution in giving him assignments resulted in important advantages for nonfamily managers when the time came to select new company leaders:

"They (the family) were keen not to push me into a situation where I might fail. When you have never been put into a position where you can fail—and you have not had a great deal of executive responsibility—there is a 'Catch-22' situation. This is a large public business and a family member who is considered for a promotion has to have been seen to succeed. The funny thing is, the majority of the work force would probably rather have a family member at the top because they have come to associate it with the basic fundamentals of the business, and the principles by which it is run."

On the other hand, even impressive qualifications can create difficulties for a younger family member where there is an obvious generation or culture gap. A director of a U.S. company described his experience:

"I was a director of a company that had been founded by my father. The individual who succeeded him had been doing a poor job for some time and the company's performance reflected that fact.

"Although I was a Harvard Law School graduate and nearly 40, I had a great deal of difficulty persuading the directors, one of whom was not much older than I, that the president was the cause of the problem. One of them even told me that I did not know how business works. The older members thought at first that my demand for the president's resignation was too radical. The younger one was intensely competitive and seldom acknowledged that I was right, even when the others did.

"We finally fired the president. When we did, I think that there was more sympathy for him than for the shareholders or other employees who had suffered because of his incompetence. If anyone else had been his major critic, he might have been let go sooner."

The heir to a Mexican manufacturing company had a similar problem when he quit a teaching job at a business school to work for the family firm. He recalled that his two uncles and many of the company's long-standing employees did not cooperate with his efforts to institute sophisticated management practices. He noted: "When I asked someone to do something, they would call my uncles first and see if they could not get some support for doing things the way they had been done in the past.''

A third case, involving a U.S. garment manufacturer, depicts this chasm in more emphatic terms. This particular heir, a Harvard Business School graduate, described his problems when he went to work for his father's company:

"We had a management that was not exactly attuned to traveling in the Philippines. They were unsophisticated. There was nobody aside from my father who had ever been outside the United States. As the nature of the business became more international, I needed to send the manufacturing people who were from New York and Philadelphia to these kinds of places. And for these guys, Tennessee and Alabama were foreign countries.''

Confronted with continued resistance between the new order and the old, with a disparity in education and cosmopolitanism between the entrenched management and the promoter of a new strategy, some sell out. In this particular case, although the company continued to be highly successful, this individual eventually elected to sell the firm.